Dear Friend,

I feel as if I know you. I have talked to you in the line at the store. I have watched you sit alone at the park while your children play. I have heard your story on the soccer sidelines. We have passed in the grocery line, with babies tied to our hips and teenagers asking for the keys to drive home. I see you. I hear you and I get it.

Motherhood, in every season, is hard—and I do not believe we should do this alone.

The repetitive work of everyday investment seems more like servanthood than an accumulation of earnings or rewards for the commitment and diligence. The truth is that most anything worth investing in will require us to become low in order to rise up. And when I rise up in my efforts in motherhood, I want them to mean something. To matter. To not just be an offering, but a sacrifice. That is what we do with gifts. We use them. We treasure them. And we give them over to God.

Surrendering our desires and our hearts to His will allow God to turn those seeds of trust into the fruit of His plan. He begins to grow our minds toward motherhood. When I surrendered my ideals, God grew a new and amazing desire and planted it within me. Full of passion and fervor, I discovered a love for what I was being called to and an understanding that every woman is given a mother's heart. We are asked to surrender ideals and embrace this high calling.

We are called to be sowers. Planting seeds, bending low, tilling the ground, sifting the dirt, pruning, watering, and weeding. It takes time and hard work to plant and reap a harvest. We need one another if we are to remember to continue to work with an end in sight, even when life seems fruitless or desperate. The heart and understanding we take into womanhood will affect our vision, our purpose, and our outcome. We don't need to suffer through God's calling on our lives.

Read that again. **Motherhood is not a call to suffer through.**

Motherhood matters because you matter. Your struggles matter, your questions matter, and your dreams matter. Embracing motherhood doesn't require you to give up the passions God has given to you. Motherhood does not destine us for drudgery and loneliness.

It is my prayer that you will find hope and help as we walk together through many motherhood matters. And that you will discover that you matter. Every woman has a mother's heart. A beautiful place from which we give, nurture, mentor, love, and dream. Let's grow those places together as we invest in others the gifts God has given us.

We have a divine purpose and the plan has already been laid out for us. Every word, action, decision, and every training moment is a part of that plan. Everything has a why. Even motherhood. It has not been lost on our feelings of inadequacy, fears of failure, or drudgeries in the mundane.

Go easy on yourself, mama. God has the big picture. And let me tell you, it is a mighty beautiful thing to behold!

September

Chapter 1: {Why} Everyone Else
Is Having a Baby & I'm Not

Are you in a season of waiting? What prayers are you waiting for God to answer?

Take a few moments to write down the dreams you have in your heart.

Write a prayer to God about where you're at right now. Are there hopes and dreams you need to surrender to Him? Use this time and space to do that.

"Motherhood captures us with a grip of commitment—with the call to be willing to release.
Do not lose heart or let go too soon. The waiting is the mystery. The giving is the gift."

Chapter 2: {Why} Dreams are Never Really Buried, and Faith is Resurrected

Are there dreams you have had to let go of or say good-bye to? Take some time to list those dreams and see if your heart has truly healed over those losses over time. No matter whether a dream is big or small, we might still mourn it.

Do you have a friend who is walking through loss? Think of women in your life who have lost a baby or may never be able to carry their own. How can you come alongside them? Have you ever asked them to share their story with you? How do you respond to this difficult time in a friend's life, and how can you walk with them through it?

Have you shared your story of loss with someone else? If so, what happened when you did? Have you come to a place where you feel God has healed this empty space so you can minister into another woman's life?

Are you afraid to talk about the release? The pain, the emotion, and the struggle? If so, why?

Did you feel inadequate to comfort another woman in the release of her dreams?

Chapter 3: {Why} Overwhelmed Does Not Have to Be Your Middle Name

Take a few minutes to reflect on the season of motherhood you're in right now.

Do you need to wave the white flag high for help? Take a few moments to present your need to God. Write down a few moms you are friends with or who you admire and could ask for help.

Have you moved beyond survival mode and are feeling relief? Take a few moments to ask God who you can come alongside in their mothering journey. Does anyone come to mind? Write their names in this space. If no one comes to mind, does your church have a mentoring ministry or a group for young moms with mentor moms? Take the steps to find out about getting involved.

QUESTIONS TO DEFINE YOUR MOTHERHOOD VISION:

PURPOSE:

When I consider the grown-up version of my children, what do I see for their future?

When I consider what God calls us to be as Christ-followers, how does this fit into my children's future?

Use your answers to create a vision for motherhood. Consider how the values and the character you know for your children's future will fit into their everyday life.

Write your Motherhood Vision here:

PRIORITIES:

These are the areas that will be foundational to your children and their future.

Pure in Heart: The {Why} of what you and your children do every day

Peacemakers: How you and your children handle conflict and resolution

Time: How your time is spent, for whom and for what (eternal perspectives, responsibility, investments)

Character: Developing good and godly character will happen in every single decision, reaction and moment of our everyday living. From healthy living choices, friendships, speech, chores and focus…all choices that will require character investment and application.

SCHEDULING:

When you find your schedule full of things that have no bearing on the purpose for your motherhood, then you have lost your vision. It may be time to re-organize your day to day life and get back to the basics.

What does this look like?

Lay out a plan for more investment and application of character development. This is not a crash course, and your children will have plenty of opportunity to apply what they are learning.

Schedule around consistency. Regular quiet time, at home time, family meals, study, music, art, health, fitness and ministry will keep everyone moving at a pretty fast pace. Consider a rotation of seasons for those areas and find a balance for everyone. Mom is usually the last one to be considered and the first to suffer the fall-out.

Make time for yourself.

Don't be afraid to ask for help.

Let some things go. Or many things.

Don't compare to other families. Their vision will be different than yours.

Remind your family of your family mission statement. If you do not have one, it may be time to create one.

THE MCCARTHY FAMILY MISSION

Live intentionally

Serve and bless others sacrificially

Keeping the boundaries of our convictions,
time and unity as a family close and true

Invest into relationships

Listen to the heart beat of others, responding
to God's call on our own lives

See others through God's eyes

Remember our family values and not expect others
to understand those, but to accept the mission statement of others as the body of Christ

Learn to listen

Stay in the Word of God, so that we may
connect the truth to all we may face

Putting others before ourselves

Distributors of grace

"Your overwhelmed is God's opportunity to amaze you."

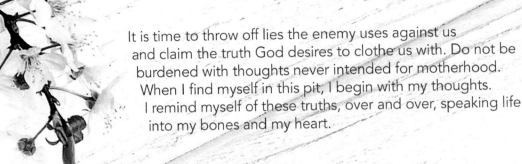

Life-Speaking Truths

It is time to throw off lies the enemy uses against us
and claim the truth God desires to clothe us with. Do not be
burdened with thoughts never intended for motherhood.
When I find myself in this pit, I begin with my thoughts.
I remind myself of these truths, over and over, speaking life
into my bones and my heart.

- God created me and has equipped me for this purpose.

- I will not believe lies based on the emotions of my circumstances in the moment.

- There are truths in the Word and from other women I need to remember right now.

- I will put off the negative response and put on loving thoughts.

- God has a unique plan for this circumstance and though I may not know what it is, I will respond with an open mind and let my emotions take back seat until I can respond correctly.

- My heart is too tender to handle this hurt or the weight of all that is before me. I will choose to see this problem as small and God as big.

- The big picture cannot be lost on everything before me.

- I will begin with one new habit today that will break this situation into smaller manageable tasks.

- What will I put off today and tomorrow, to find balance between what is expected and what is needed?

- Have I reached out for advice, help, or care when I need it?

- What will my one new habit be per week to help me find myself at peace with my motherhood?

- What is pushing my buttons? The list of things I need to do, or my inability to find a way out from around it?

When our minds are fixed on the truth, everything else comes into focus.

Write your motherhood vision from the last chapter in this space:

If you understand your purpose, it's easier to set boundaries. Keep your motherhood vision in front of you daily. Write it on a chalkboard or whiteboard. Type it up in a beautiful font, print it, and hang it somewhere you will see regularly—in a frame or on your refrigerator.

I have gathered a few ideas to help you choose what may be best. Filter your choices, your thoughts, and your scheduled priorities through these four simple measures of how a decision serves your purpose and God's purpose for you.

Accountability: Does this choice follow God's Word and a trusted mentor's wisdom?

Timing: Can something new fit into the bigger and best picture?

Vision: Am I making choices that align with my vision and purpose?

Focus: Am I remaining steadfast in keeping top priorities and valuable investments first in thought and action?

Discover your pushing points and emotional responses by asking yourself, is it always the same child, circumstance or conditions that cause me to react this way?

"When you say no to the right things, every good thing comes into focus."

Daily Practices to Become
Less Overwhelmed and More Amazed

- Before you put your feet on the floor in the morning, pray and keep praying.

- Make your bed. Make it pretty.

- Give yourself permission to enjoy the moments, rather than seeing everything as a task.

- Act—don't react.

- Take something off your to-do list that can wait.

- Go for a walk, even if you need to take your children.

- Get in the Word. Get your family in the Word.

- If you do nothing else: Rest and love your family.

- Tell your family how much you love them. Don't just show them.

Find one spot and moment for quiet time and free time. Guilt free!

Always bring moments back to the Lord. Even spilled cereal.

- Celebrate your wins and shake off your mistakes.

- Give yourself grace and prayer time to make the big decisions.

- Claim God's truth over the lies you may hear.

- Memorize one verse a day. Write it on your heart.

- Smile. Let your family see you smile.

- Let your no stand on its own. You don't need to list all the reasons you've declined.

- Give someone the blessing of helping you.

- Put your family first, even when it comes to ministry opportunities.

- Avoid lumping all your problems, to-do lists, and responsibilities into one emotional pile.

Get to know the women around you. Give them your hand, your heart, and your honesty. Invite them in. Let's skim the overwhelming right off the top of the motherhood cup we fill every day, and be there for one another—before we are running on empty.

Take a moment to think about the women around you—in your church or neighborhood, in your child's school or activities—that you would like to get to know. Write their names in this space.

We are sometimes oblivious to the barrier between the generations and the gaps that have caused women to not extend themselves into one another's lives. What are the barriers keeping you from connecting with the women you listed above?

We can begin retraining our vision, our mind-set, and our daily practices in our relationships to connect, to encourage, and to gather. Here are a few ideas to help you begin:

- Say hello to someone new at Church this week.

- Offer to help another mom at the store. Load her groceries, say something encouraging, tell her to keep up the good work. Or, perhaps you may need to ask someone else for help. Reach out and let your inhibitions fall aside.

- Look for the women around you who seem to be doing life alone. Reach out to them with a visit or a card.

- Visit the nursing home and listen to someone else's story.

- Take the time to consider those that you may be comparing yourself to. Reach out and ask this person how they are.

- When you are in a group of women this week, stop to listen. Really listen. Often we forget that everyone else has a life that could be just as busy and complicated as ours.

Write down what you will do this week to break down those barriers and get to know one of the women you listed above.

"I refuse to make motherhood about me. I refuse to compare myself to other women.
I refuse to take the credit for what God is doing."

Chapter 6: {Why} We Need to Let Them In

The biggest first step for any woman is to let others in. But where do we go from there? How does this look in real life and off the page? Here are a few simple questions to ask yourself to determine what letting others in might look like for you.

FOR THE YOUNGER MOTHER

What is keeping you from reaching out for help or allowing someone to be a part of the messy parts of your life?

When women begin to draw closer and ask questions, do you shy away or put up walls?
If so, why?

Do you feel that the older generation may judge you or meet you with condemnation rather than grace in their efforts to be helpful?

Have you experienced the sweet blessing of another woman coming alongside you and lending a hand? If you have, how did that make you feel? If not, who can you turn to for help and fellowship?

Are you able to put your own ideas and judgements aside to walk with another mother in grace and patience? If not, what's holding you back? If so, what can you do differently?

Do you ever feel that you "have done your time," and this generation can figure it out just like you had to? What does this generation need that fits what God has prepared you to give?

Have you felt a resistance or a wall from the younger generations that perhaps they do not need or want what you might have to offer? What was that like?

What would be a practical, grace-filled way for you to let other women know you are there for them?

"It takes practice to receive well. It's a daily giving back to the Lord and a lesson in learning how to let others into our lives."

Chapter 7: {Why} We Can Learn to Love Our Children Uniquely

Take some time today to identify your child(ren)'s love language(s) and your own.

HOW TO DISCOVER YOUR CHILD'S PRIMARY LOVE LANGUAGE

1. Observe how your child expresses love to you.

2. Observe how your child expresses love to others.

3. Listen to what your child requests most often.

4. Notice what your child most frequently complains about.

5. Give your child a choice between two options.

Is there a child in my home or already grown who I struggle to understand?

Do I have a disconnection in communication or understanding with one of my children that is disruptive to our home?

Have I taken the time to invest in speaking my child's love language, or do I find it difficult to embrace those differences?

Am I missing out on receiving my child's love because I am waiting expectantly for my own needs to be met?

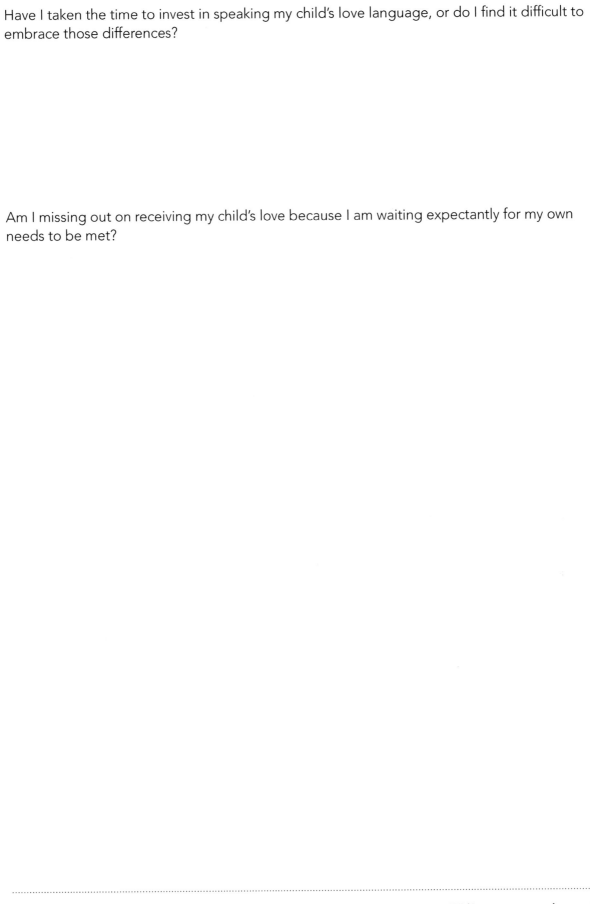

"Finding your children's strengths and love languages is like mining for gold. While you are panning and sifting to find their gifts and talents and help them grow, you discover the way to their hearts."

Chapter 8: {Why} Your Children Can Learn to Love One Another Well

I know exactly what some of you may be thinking right now. It would take a miracle to have one day of peace in this home. If just one day is all you are asking, then, let's begin there and consider the steps we can take to get the ball rolling.

It's important to prepare helpful and practical ideas that will pull your family together when the struggle to step away is real. Here are some ideas our family turns to when we have a new concept, plan, or an important matter we all need to discuss. Try putting them into practice as you plan your one day of peace:

- ✏ Have a family meeting. Seriously, this is a real thing. Your family will most likely laugh at you the first time you call for a meeting as a group, but you will walk away hooked. It might take time for everyone to loosen up and get used to the idea of sharing their ideas and emotions as a group, but this is where honesty and trust grows in all of you.

FAMILY MEETING BASICS 101

1. Structure

   a. Length of time will vary: Depending on age and purpose in meeting

   b. Begin with the reason for the meeting (conflict leading up to, need for a change, planning purposes)

   c. Parent leads meeting, allowing everyone a turn to contribute

   d. Communication is to be kind, open, honest and tempered

   e. Planning meetings are to be met with open minds and contribution to ideas

   f. Meetings for change or conflict resolution should be met with acceptance and willingness to work together

2. Prepare

   a. Consider ages of your family and plan accordingly

   b. Think outside of your emotion when considering what to say

   c. Remember your family can be the strongest unit any of you have, and this meeting will be the foundation to your future

   d. Write out your ideas to keep meeting on track

3. Gather your family for a talk

    a. Depending on ages and stages, you may have to "require" everyone to be present

    b. Set the time and place (living room, kitchen table, etc.)

    c. Be prepared ahead of time with your "agenda" and "purpose"

    d. Don't forget to pray

4. Assemble and Explain

    a. The first meeting will be laying the groundwork

    b. You (and/or your spouse) will open your family meeting with the Family Meeting Concept

    c. Explain your plan to hold regular, mandatory family meetings

    d. Let everyone talk and share ideas

    e. Remember some meetings will be for authority purpose and some will be for conversation

    f. Pray together

5. Lay the "ground rules"

    a. No interrupting

    b. Listening

    c. Asking questions

    d. Understanding the need for a resolution

    e. Commitment

6. Follow-through

    a. Every meeting should have a final resolution

    b. Parent(s) should be committed to follow-through

    c. Plan another meeting if there needs to be accountability, apologies, more planning or support

ᴥ Introduce the Four Rules of Communication to your family and explain that they will be your "go to" for every word or conversation that you speak to one another.

1. Be honest

2. Keep current—don't focus on the past

3. Attack the problem, not the person

4. Act—don't react

- Talk about what the Bible speaks about love. For example: "Love is patient" (1 Corinthians 13:4 NIV). Take one attribute or action like this from the Bible, and have everyone practice it every day for one week. At the end of the week, ask, "Were we patient to one another this week? How and when?" Be sure to praise good behavior and character. Then move onto the next attribute.

- Discuss how to handle conflict. Cover the principle that we are responsible for our own words, actions, and reactions.

"Love begins in the home. If you cannot love your family well, then how will you love others?"

Be The Change

> Be in the Word of God daily.

> Overflow with the goodness God gives you.

> Fill your home with music, art, literature, and fun.

> Smile.

> Discourage arguing and complaining.

> Avoid gossip and don't be a Debbie Downer.

> Keep a schedule and spend time together.

> Learn to love one another well.

> Be creative and fill your home with laughter.

Four Family Rules to Better Communication

1. Be honest
2. Keep current—don't focus on the past
3. Attack the problem, not the person
4. Act—don't react

Chapter 9: {Why} You Should
Love Your Spouse More Than Your Kids

When the builder and I became a true team, the change was evident to our children. It drastically changed our parenting and our model of loving. If there is one word to clearly define the instrument of our beginnings together, our restart, it is this: humility.

Every one of us is inclined to lose sight of that which is most important in our lives. Often those things that matter the most to us get in the way of our first loves. The builder and I created this list to keep us in check when we find ourselves feeling separated by distractions. As you go through your day, answer the questions and take the action steps. Soon you will notice the difference, and so will your kids.

LOVING TOGETHER CHECKLIST

- ✓ Am I functioning off my own to-do lists daily?
- ✓ Have we lost our vision as a couple?
- ✓ Kiss every day. In front of the children.
- ✓ Do we communicate about our needs and desires more than business as usual?
- ✓ Are we working as a team in our parenting?
- ✓ Go to bed together at the same time.
- ✓ Always say I'm sorry in current time.
- ✓ Remember that we are both changing.
- ✓ Learn to love the new.
- ✓ Never stop talking.
- ✓ Be available to each other at all times.

Marriage will have seasons of momentum and seasons of moving through life together, but the most important thing to purpose together, is to make one another a priority.

Identify your greatest challenges to finding the time to invest into your marriage. (Work, children, ministry, distractions, health, etc.)

Consider a few of the date night ideas below to making your marriage a focus for your future:

- Take turns planning

- Commit to weekly

- Consider dating at home if your circumstances restrict you from leaving once in a while

- Get healthy and stay healthy together

- Allow work to take a back seat

- Date with a purpose

"When your focus is online on motherhood, you can and will sideline your spouse."

Chapter 10: {Why} Raising Responsible Children Requires Work

If you're feeling overwhelmed with what it might take for your child to become responsible, it might be time to take a deep breath and roll up your sleeves. Here are some small steps to take. These probably won't happen overnight and will probably be more for you than your child. I promise every ounce of effort you put in now will reap a lifetime of benefits for everyone. Take time to talk to the Lord and be in the Word before you dive in to raise a more responsible child. It is going to take you and God.

LET'S BEGIN HERE

Identify the areas in your child's life where you would like to see them grow.

Ask a friend or family member to point out areas of responsibility where they see your child needs teaching and ownership.

Begin listing the jobs, tasks, or details you may be taking care of for your child that they can take responsibility for themselves.

Make a plan and work on one new thing a week or month, depending on your child.

Ask yourself why you have not started this process before.

- ⤺ Was I aware of their lack of responsibility?

- ⤺ Was it easier to do those things myself?

- ⤺ Do I feel as if my child should not have to help, work, or have accountability as a child?

- ⤺ Do I empathize with my child's whining and tears or is it too difficult to deal with their stubborn or lazy behavior?

List creative ideas to motivate your child and consequences for a lack of follow-through.

Ask yourself: Will I lose heart in this endeavor easily, and should I get someone else on board to keep me accountable throughout the year?

Ask yourself: Do I fully realize my child will grow into a selfish adult if I do not work on this area now?

WHAT'S NEXT?

Begin teaching your children character that counts. The root of all responsibility is good character and unselfish desires.

Make a plan that works for your family. Create charts, checklists, character lessons, accountability plans, and daily chore checks.

Remind yourself that it will be easy to give in and allow a privilege to a child who has not shown responsibility. The hard part is the follow-through and consistent expectations. You will need to train, teach, show, and revisit responsibility in so many areas. Our children will need to see, touch, hear, and be taught what responsibility looks like.

You can find various resources for Character lessons and Chore Checks at **SeptemberMcCarthy.com**. I also recommend **CharacterFirstEducation.com**

"A hardworking child grows into a responsible adult."

Chapter 11: {Why} The Yelling Mom
Can Find Hope and Help

Read through these points and circle the ones you most need to claim. Write them on a 3x5 card and carry them with you this week to allow God to breathe hope into these times. Welcome that transformation with an open heart.

- ↙ We are all sinners. I should not be surprised when I display my weakness and weariness in this way.

- ↙ God died for this: To give me power, strength, and victory over all through redemption (1 Corinthians 6:14). I need to claim this.

- ↙ Regret will only lead to change through repentance. I should never be too proud to apologize to my children and ask for their forgiveness.

- ↙ I have the power of the written Word. I will memorize Scripture about the tongue. About the influence of words. About anger and about true love.

- ↙ I will learn to walk away. When I feel the tension in a conversation with my children or a situation that I am completely bewildered by, I will walk away. (This might feel strange, but it can help you to gather your senses and God's peace in the moment.) If I need to leave my kids standing there wondering where I disappeared to for a few minutes, then this is what I'll do.

- ↙ If my child's actions are disrespectful, challenging, or disobedient, and I don't feel that I can handle the situation with the appropriate reaction, then I will ask them to leave the room or I will remove myself from the situation.

- ↙ I will recognize my boundaries, weaknesses, and points of frustration and begin working through those to identify the real reason I am bothered. Is it exhaustion, selfishness, or a lack of training in my children that might be causing the troubling moments?

- ↙ Yelling is not an option. If I work on my heart and the triggers to my frustrations, then my tone and reactions will transform. Identifying my triggers and modifying my responses will require an investment daily.

- ↙ There is no power greater than the Word of God and His authority. With prayer, memorization, and His strength, I can find victory in this area of my life.

- ↙ Little daily changes become big life habits. There is always hope.

"When we barely recognize who we have become, this is the perfect time to let God transform us."

Chapter 12: {Why} You Need to Throw Mom Guilt Out the Window

WHAT I DO FOR MY FAMILY IN A DAY	WHAT I WISH I COULD DO FOR THEM

Look at your lists. Put a check next to the areas that are focused on happiness for your children. Now circle the areas that are focused on their godliness and growth. Do you see the extra, unnecessary weight and burden you have taken on because of guilt? Sure, there are things we cannot remove from our everyday responsibilities, but we heap on more than we need to do and feel the guilt if we do not quite measure up to our own standards. Consider whether the list of things you didn't accomplish is actually a list of important efforts toward godliness and growth or whether they are merely undone tasks that add more guilt and mental stress.

What are you doing or owning for your children that they could be doing for themselves?

Make a comprehensive list of the areas of motherhood that usher in stress.

Now write out a prayer giving those areas of stress to God and asking Him to help you focus on the important aspects of raising your child(ren).

"For every little part of your child's life you try to own and fix for them, you are taking away something from the work and worth of God in their lives."

Chapter 13: {Why} Interrupting, Whining, and Complaining Don't Have to Control Your Home

Motherhood is hard enough. Then add in a lot of extra and unnecessary noise on top of the workload? It seems we would be desperate to eliminate those things that we could fix. Some things take years of investment and work to see a harvest, and then there are those things like interrupting, whining, and complaining, which can see almost immediate results.

Start today by teaching your children how to calmly come alongside you and make their presence known by placing their hand at your hip and awaiting your hand to be placed atop their own. The more you practice this with them, the more confident they will feel to do this when you are speaking to others out in public or at home.

To help your family discover new ways of communicating that don't involve whining and complaining, create a list of words and phrases that build up and a list of those that tear down. When the language in the house is becoming negative, remind everyone of the positive words. Make it a fun household challenge to use only the uplifting words. Every great habit starts with practice!

- Thank you for dinner, mom.
- I will try better next time.
- May I make an appeal?
- No, thank you.
- I would be happy to.
- Excuse me.
- May I help you?
- How do you feel today?

"Give your children a reason to change and the symptoms will improve.
Give them something to change for."

How can we be at peace with our kids' choices, cry in quiet over their pain, and wait for their listening hearts to find their way?

- We pray without ceasing.

- We cry out with our pleas, anger, and our confusion with humility.

- We give God control.

- We tell God our woes.

Take some time to bow low and give God your motherhood on the altar as a sacrifice. Use this space to pour out your heart to Him.

"Your most worthy moments in motherhood will be on your knees."

When we identify our pursuits, we realize our passions. If living a life of faith has not become a part of your routine or habits, this is the time to make some changes.

Take a look at your schedule or daily routine. Where is your time going? What priorities do you see? Is God currently a priority for you and your family or more of an afterthought?

If your faith is not currently a priority in your family's rhythms, what can you do to change that this week? What can you do to focus on God daily? To teach your children about Him? To model a life of walking with Him?

"God fills in the gaps. But we want our kids to know who He is before that inevitable day arrives."

Chapter 16: {Why} A Mother in the Word Can Lead Her Family Well

Let's begin together, right now, right here, to lead our families well. Will you take five minutes to read through a few of the verses I'm about to share here with you? I have read, reread, and applied these scriptures to my motherhood for many years. What a wonderful place to begin—right where God can meet you every day in the life that you have chosen to make matter. He is the Great Provider and Sustainer, so let Him use these verses to be an encouragement to you as you begin to see the value of just five minutes in His truths. Let your time expand with your heart. Remember, your time seeking God will forever change the future of your motherhood.

TOPIC	SCRIPTURE
My Choices	Psalm 1
My Spiritual Growth Exam	Psalm 4
Focus on the Future	Psalm 16
Prayer and Praise	Psalm 27:14, Psalm 28:7, Psalm 31:7, Psalm 100
Desire for God	Psalm 42
Help and Comfort	Psalm 46
Pour Out Your Heart	Psalm 62
Prayers for Our Children	Psalm 78
Knowing Christ During Crisis	Psalm 86
God's Love and Our Response	Psalm 103
My Christian Walk	Matthew 5
Everyday Faith	Hebrews 11
Living Out My Faith	James
My Tongue	James 3
My Walk with God	1 Peter
Seek His Face	Psalm 105:4-5
Seeking True Wisdom	Proverbs
Call-to-Action	Proverbs 4
Slowing Humility and Righteousness	Proverbs 10-11

Yielding Fruit	Proverbs 12
Tongue of the Wise Woman	Proverbs 13-14
Soft Answers	Proverbs 15:1
Committing Our Work and Wisdom to God	Proverbs 16
Our Words	Proverbs 16:24-25
Considering My Actions	Matthew 7
Judging	Matthew 18
My Responsibility	Matthew 22:37-40
My Calling	Luke 3:4-6
While We Work for God	Romans 8
Practical Christian Living	Romans 12
Edification	Romans 15
Joy and Thankfulness	Philippians
Perseverance	2 Corinthians 4
My Salvation in Action	Ephesians 2
Communication	Ephesians 4
Armor of God for the Everyday Battle	Ephesians 6
Contentment	Philippians 4
Rejoicing in the Lord	Philippians 4
Motherhood	Colossians 3
Faithfulness	1 Thessalonians 5
Memory Work	John 1, Romans 12, James 1, Matthew 5, Psalm1

"Your time seeking God will forever change the future of your motherhood."

Is it time for you to own your personal role in giving the Word of God to your children in bite-sized portions?

What do you feel you need to do to get this rolling and make it your own?

You don't need to feel intimidated. It's always best to start with a plan. When will you have your family devotions? Will it be at the breakfast or dinner table? Another time during the day?

Read through the Bite Sized Beginnings list on the following page and choose where you will start today.

"God's Word is not intimidating. It is our fear of not bringing it alive for our children that stalls us. God's Word is quick and active (Hebrews 4:12). He will do the work. Just lead in obedience."

Bite Sized Beginnings

- Choose one verse per week to memorize as a family.

- After steady progress, begin adding more verses into your memory time.

- Make up hand motions for your memory verses.

- Use rhythms, songs, flashcards, or other creative ideas to help the words stick.

Sing out of a praise book or a hymnal or listen to a worship CD.

- Use age-appropriate devotional study Bibles for your children.

- Start small and add more time and content as you and they are comfortable.

- Add in Bible trivia.

- Add in "Sword Drills" (a simple contest search for verses) as a family.

- Always read from your Bible, even when using other materials.

- Repeat verses for emphasis.

- Ask questions and give your children practical application ideas.

- Have your children read verses out loud.

- Talk about a verse that encourages serving others. Then do ministry as a family.

Use nature as a catalyst for your topic choices.

- Use a conflict in your home as a study from the Word.

- Be flexible with your timing but consistent with your commitment.

- Give little ones grace and wiggle room. Let them enjoy time in the Word.

- Illustrate and color the Bible stories and display the art.

- Use holidays to spend more time in focused passages of Scripture.

- Keep journals and encourage your children to journal and take notes.

- Help them find passages in their own Bibles and ask them to follow along.

- Use maps to learn where Bible stories take place.

- Get your kids moving; it will help the learning process.

To raise children who will know how to seek God and the wisdom of others, we can be the example to them in our motherhood. Here are some guidelines and truths I found to be helpful:

Let others in. Often we doubt the intentions of others and our skepticism or mistrust puts up walls that may need tearing down. Pray that God will give you the ability and discernment to allow others to help you, bear your burdens, and give you wisdom.

Be real and raw. When someone asks how you are, answer them with grace-filled honesty. Not everyone needs to know the nitty-gritty details, but we can tell them the truth. What is the truth of how you are doing right now?

Genuine people will show they care. If you are struggling with trusting those around you with the reality of your struggles, questions, or exhaustion, then use this as a discerning tool to help you form a pattern of sharing your burdens with others. Who in your life reciprocates your honesty with prayer, help, verses, wisdom, or confirmation?

Do not hide your reality from your children. Is there a reality you need to share with your kids right now?

Consider your children and their ages. You know your children better than anyone.

- 5 and Under: It is okay for your children to see you cry, to hear your prayers and to know you are working on some hard things.

- 6-10: Speak truth to your children so they understand your need for help, for change or rest. Give them the opportunity to help. They are not too little for this and it is not a burden for them.

- 11-18: Reality for your children now is what you allow them to know and not just see. They can learn so much, grow and mature in your own journey. Let them see God work in the details and don't be afraid to let them see you pray and work through the challenges together.

Do not expect your children to understand. Your children won't understand the full scope of the concerns you face as an adult, but that isn't the lesson and wisdom they are supposed to glean from you. The spiritual growth will occur when they see you in your weakest moments, giving everything to God and allowing Him to show His supernatural strength in your lives. Honesty is the open door to growth.

What do you have to hide? If you're trying to cover your tired eyes, your weary bones, and your words with something other than the truth, what will your children know about life and leaning into Jesus?

The tired mom can be the most influential mom, because God shines His redemption in everything through a lens of honesty and truth. Mama, please do not hide your financial stress, your long, tired nights, or your worry over the future from your children. I used to feel like I was complaining and grumbling and this would be all my children ever remembered of me. I was reminded that a truly strong and brave woman will let others in and allow God to shine His will and redemption in her life. My influence depends on my honesty.

"There is so much grace afforded to us, but we often miss it because we have confused independence with strength. God gives us strength, and we can rely on others to bear our burdens when we cannot."

Chapter 19: {Why} Our Children Should Serve (Even When It's Uncomfortable)

How are you modeling service to your children? Are there ministries you were involved in before having kids that you aren't now? Is there a way for you to include your children in that ministry?

Here are some ideas to help you and your family get started:

- Create handwritten notes for neighbors, family members, or strangers.
- Deliver kindness (baked goods, notes, flowers) to others.
- Practice random acts of kindness.
- Serve in church ministries.
- Carry groceries for others.
- Read to the elderly.
- Put carts away in parking lots.
- Visit nursing homes.
- Use unique gifts to minister to others (music, art, talking, baking, reading).
- Learn to pray at home and in public for others.

What other ideas do you have for getting your family involved in serving?

Choose one of the ideas above and set a date in the next week or so to serve as a family.

"It is my job to show my children what the hands and feet of Jesus look like. When I encourage my children to serve with their strengths and their weaknesses, it allows them to see that anyone who has given his or her life to Him can serve."

{39}

When was the last time you stepped outside your comfort zone to listen to God's leading to follow and serve Him?

Where can you minister locally? In our day-to-day lives, we lose sight of the needs around us. We have a wide-open canvas of opportunity right in front of us. It can be as simple as making a meal for a family with a new baby or illness. Baking cookies to brighten the day of a neighbor. Helping an elderly person with yardwork or paying them a visit.

How can we serve the Lord as a family while in this season of life?

"I have learned not to listen to reason when it comes to serving."

We often mistake our time spent teaching as just another sacrifice for our children, but really, we are the ones blessed in the end. The benefits of teaching Scripture to your children far outweigh the time and work you will put in when they are young.

Don't forget that you are learning right along with them, and every verse you have put to memory or covered with your kiddos is another morsel of wisdom to draw from when correcting character, addressing behavior, or encouraging your kids daily. This time also reaps the benefit of applying it to your own lives. The Word of the Lord is alive and active. It comes back to your mind, from the recesses of your memory, when you need it. I can promise you it will never return void.

Let's begin small. I like to use the approach of breaking Scripture into smaller portions. The chart on the next page is just a suggested plan and a starting point for your kids. This will look different for every family, but the key is application. Remember, knowledge alone puffs up, but knowledge with the love and wisdom of Christ will transform.

"There is no greater gift to give your children than to hide God's Word in their hearts."

	Weekly Work	Application	Song/Music	Rhymes	Hand Motions	Flashcards	Repetition	Sign Language	Other Tools
Matthew 5:1-11									
1 John 1									
Fruit of the Spirit									
Armor of God									
Books of the Old Testament									
Books of the New Testament									
James 1									
Romans 12									
Psalm 1									
Matthew 6:33									
Matthew 7:12									
John 3:16									
John 14:6									
Proverbs 15:1									
Proverbs 3:1-11									
Psalm 119:1-3									
Psalm 23									
Psalm 34:14									
Galatians 5:22-23									

Chapter 22: {Why} We Don't Want to Raise Robots

I am excited to see us run this race together in the years to come. I see your children growing right up and alongside my own. I see you learning their strengths and building up their weaknesses. I am championing you as you learn your parenting ruts and ridiculous rules (believe me, we all have them), and as you grow champions who love and live differently than others. We are a team, and so is your family. Here are two next steps to take to build your family team and to honor the individuals who make up that team.

1. We can begin by getting to know our children. I am not referring to being able to list those things that annoy us or the areas in which we think they could do better or aren't living up to our expectations.

   Set aside time this week (or in the next few weeks) to spend individual time with your child(ren). Engage in conversations with them, spend time together, ask questions, serve them, give them God, and tend to their hearts.

   Watch how your child responds, what they lean toward. Let's remember that the way our children bend is not to be swayed by our preferences, but by God's principles.

2. We will need to identify our purpose in all that we do. Most generally, mothers expect obedience and reaction to follow the words, "because I told you so." But if our children's responses to our instruction are to be respectful and timely, it is our job to remember that our expectations should meet a higher standard and not have selfish, unrealistic gain attached. We are accountable to God with our words and rules. Focus this week on raising children who are sensitive to His Word and be careful to avoid conformity.

"Motherhood is not an experiment where we cross our fingers and hope for a good outcome. We are given gifts to be grown and molded as part of God's amazing plan. The simplest yet most profound job in motherhood is to know the plan and guide children in the plan."

Chapter 23: {Why} It's Okay to Say No to Your Children

Answer these questions to determine if you are parenting for temporary peace or for lasting impact:

Do I feel uncomfortable giving my children boundaries or consequences to their actions?

Would I recognize disrespect in my children?

Do I wait until I feel the pushing points before I choose to handle a problem?

Am I more longsuffering, and do I tend to ignore a problem until it escalates out of hand?

What tangible daily practices am I implementing at home (or could I implement at home) to help train my children away from poor choices and behavior?

Chapter 24: {Why} Can't Means Won't, So Do the Hard Things

Give your children the tools to do the hard things for God:

- Identify their identity in Christ and their gifts from God.

- Awaken their hearts and minds to their potential.

- Find outlets for them to put their gifts to good use.

- Pray Scripture and God's truth over them.

- Teach your children what sacrifice is, for hard things do not come easily.

- Train your children to be diligent and consistent.

- Give your children the gift of communication. Teach them how to use their words wisely.

- Always come back to the why of their strengths.

- Cheer on excellence and not perfection.

- Pray for humility: Character training will be the biggest factor in helping your children thrive in their strengths.

- Require practice over laziness.

- Model balance and perseverance.

- Encourage them to serve with their strengths.

- Teach your children to seek and praise the Giver and not the gifts.

- Don't be afraid to believe God has a big plan for your child.

- Pray with your children over their weaknesses and their strengths.

- Remind them that can't means won't.

Read through the list above and put a check mark next to the things you are already doing in your home. Look at the remaining items and write below the 3 you want to focus on implementing in your home.

What will you do this week to start these practices?

"Motherhood is not about raising perfect children in the sight of man, or settling for comfortable when we can be more. I want my children to know more of God and less of themselves; then their weaknesses will be in His strength."

Chapter 25: {Why} We Hope to Answer
Their Tough Questions

I want to champion you in this area over and over because it will take practice and brave, intentional steps into your children's safe spaces. When they open themselves to your words, your wisdom, and your advice, it will be your job to nurture and grow this relationship uniquely.

The best way to begin is to identify the areas in which your children will need guidance and boundaries. You will never be able to predict the future, but we all surely know we can begin to plan, pray, and prepare for certain conversations. Here are a few topics you can expect to meet on your horizon of motherhood. Circle the ones that your children are facing now or may be next on the horizon.

- Modesty

- Privacy

- Friendships

- Strangers and safety

- Boundaries for exposure to pornography, violence, and crude behavior

- Social media

- Language that is hurtful or ungodly

- Bullying

- Time management and stewardship

- Puberty

- Sex

- Abstinence and purity

- Relationships and dating

- Engagement and marriage

- Future

Every day is an opportunity to build a stronger relationship and better communication skills with your child. We do not need to wait for the big talks to get into their world. Use your moments wisely. How will you begin building a stronger relationship with your child today?

Choose your words carefully, and don't allow their external circumstances and their emotional responses to affect you personally. This is my challenge every day. Ask God to help you get out of the way so you can see and hear and respond to what your children are truly communicating.

"I am challenged daily to raise truth seekers and not opinion followers. We are raising generations today."

Chapter 26: {Why} Teaching Responsibility Doesn't Have to Be Drudgery

Let's keep our minds focused on our goal, or we may feel like stopping short before our kids reach the finish line. Teaching responsibility is like passing a baton after running laps around the same track; and when you have handed it over, be prepared to be amazed. Your child will begin to own his or her life and run with it. Here are some places to begin.

Training: Identify the character traits you are going to incorporate into your child's every day and begin here.

How will you repeat and reinforce these character traits?

Consistency: Consistency is vital because someone else is always affected by our choices. Always consider the effect the opposite of our actions would have on the world around us, and we will find a motivation for every aspect of our lives. Give your children the why, so their efforts will be consistent.

What are your greatest challenges in being consistent?

What will you do this week to be more consistent?

Follow-through: We worry about all the things that would go forgotten, missing, or left undone if we didn't follow through. This doesn't mean we're going to take on everyone's lives, jobs, chores, or homework. We are just going to be intentional about bringing them along for the follow-through. When your family forgets to say thank you for hospitality shown to them, do you apologize and thank others on their behalf, or bring your children back to a point of gratefulness and verbal acknowledgement? Follow through, mom, but do not own your children's lives for them.

What areas of your child's life have you owned that you need to turn back over to them?

Mean what you say and say what you mean: Often the hardest thing for mothers to do is to follow through on quick, honest, real-life consequences once they state them. We speak with so much emotion in the midst of conflict, it is a miracle our families can even understand us at times. We declare nonsensical consequences for a lack of responsibility and find it hard to live up to our own declarations. "You are grounded for life. You cannot go out in public for a year. No youth group for a month." Where do we come up with this stuff? It is survival sparked with emotion. But, as the builder sweetly chides me, "Mean what you say and say what you mean." Carefully weigh your words and give precise instructions. Confusion muddles expectations, and a mother's emotions mixed with instruction can be confusing. Stay calm and speak life. We want to light their fire and not put it out.

Chapter 27: {Why} You Don't Need to Count to Three

To ease the transition, let's begin with a few questions to identify where you are in your motherhood journey:

Has my counting become a crutch to avoid an obedience struggle?

Will my children struggle with this concept, or will I lack the fortitude to train them consistently in obedience?

Will I be able to be consistent in training my children in first-time obedience?

Do I understand and believe in the value of this principle?

What might keep me from training my children in this area and why?

Am I thinking about the future and the more grown-up child exhibiting a lack of respect, honor, and timely obedience?

Here are a few practical First-Time Obedience Tips; the rest is up to you and consistency.

- Have a family meeting to explain how you are going to work as a team to make a few changes. Carefully explain and give examples of what first-time obedience will look like in your home. Role-play and laugh a lot.

- Start small and do not expect your child to grasp or like this new concept right away. It will take time and consistency, mixed with patience and love, to create a home characterized by first-time obedience.

- Remember the fruit of the Spirit (Galatians 5:22-23). Encourage your child to be joyful, and remember to put on your own patience and self-control.

- Follow through with consequences when your child forgets or refuses to listen.

- Celebrate obedience and continue to praise your child for trying as you continue this process.

- If you have older children, it is not too late to introduce the idea of listening with respect and honoring your instructions with a timely response. All of us can use some practice in honor and respect. Obedience is an external action of the heart. Begin today.

....

"You are on the road to revolutionizing the atmosphere in your home and the tender places of your child's heart. Obedience is an external reaction to a well-tended heart grown in respect and honor."

Have you fully surrendered your plan to the Lord? Those ideas, desires, and callings that seem to pull on you stronger than motherhood or His call on your life? This is the hardest stretching, pruning part of a fully focused life for Jesus. May I gently come alongside you in this, and encourage you that there truly is no better plan for any of our lives than the one God has already prepared? A fully focused life doesn't guarantee comfort and freedom from pain. Surrender does not mean a glorious return in the moment. Surrender is giving back what we've been given. The pull of the world can be stronger than the decision to allow our efforts to be unseen for a time. Motherhood's return has a kingdom value, and the rewards are your children's focus and future.

A few questions for reflection might help you explore where you are in your journey.

Where do my affections lie?

Am I seeking pleasure over principle?

Do I know why I make the decisions I do and what the end goal is?

What am I working toward?

Am I exhausted and storing up earthly treasures with no eternal value?

Have I ever truly surrendered the gifts God has given to me, to be used in His time and for His glory?

Was there a time I chose to give my life to God? Today is the perfect time to believe He died for me and His plan is infinitely bigger than my own.

What are my idols? Has my family replaced God on the altar of my focus and my future?

What are the influences in my life that may be determining my focus?

Do my children see my diligence and efforts as part of His plan?

How can I let go of my own control and let God have my motherhood too?

My friend, if your life seems to be in a tailspin, do not be disheartened. Let this sink deep and resonate with you today: God is on the throne. Motherhood is a daily surrender, and God sees all the hard stuff, even when no one else can. May our focus be on the One who is our strength.

You are not alone in your motherhood. If you feel your life has been robbed of excitement, your dreams, and your plans, perhaps it is time to discover the abundant life God has waiting for you. Walk with me in the truth that He will never leave you or forsake you. Even when your children move out or choose another way, you are never alone.

....

"A focused family with an eternal pursuit will produce kingdom changers for generations to come."

If you take away only one message from reading through this section, let it be this: ***Let God have your motherhood, and He will give you the joy and the reason you have been searching for.*** It will be contagious and flow over and into every area of training, teaching, and living you do with your children.

What will be the focus we give our children today? Are we truly giving them a reason to change, or just a handful of to-do's that may have a desirable outcome? Let's give them a why and let God determine the rest.

You are so loved and not alone. I wish I could send you off with a warm pumpkin muffin that my daughters now bake better than myself, and give you a hug. I hope you will know the richness of His abundant grace on your life.

Don't be afraid to tell someone your struggles, and let God have the glory in the repairs. He is the ultimate reason why motherhood matters.

September